Prayers
for
Children

Illustrated by

Janet & Anne Grahame Johnstone

Ideals Publishing Corp.

Milwaukee, Wisconsin

Copyright © MCMLXXXI by Dean & Son Ltd.
All rights reserved. Printed and bound in U.S.A.
Published simultaneously in Canada.

ISBN 0-8249-8023-9 325

BY God's fair air
I grind the grain;
Give ye good prayer
When bread ye gain.

A little old lady in a humble cot,
Said, "Jesus, thank You, for all I've got;
A tiny house and a garden plot,
To some folks it's little, to me it's a lot.

My pussy, my budgie, my mongrel Spot;
The daisies, the roses, the forget-me-not,
The rain, so fresh, the sun so hot.
Thank You, Jesus, for all I've got."

PRAISE God from Whom all blessings flow,
Praise Him, all creatures here below.
Praise Him above, the heavenly host,
Praise Father, Son and Holy Ghost

(St. John)

JESUS, tender shepherd, hear me,
  Bless Thy little lamb tonight.
Through the darkness be Thou near me,
Keep me safe till morning light.

All this day Thy hand hast led me,
And I thank Thee for Thy care.
Thou hast clothed me, warmed me, fed me,
Listen to my evening prayer.

Let my sins be all forgiven,
Bless the friends I love so well.
Take me home at last to Heaven,
Happy there with Thee to dwell.

MARY L. DUNCAN

THE Lord is my shepherd, I shall not want.
  He maketh me to lie down in green pastures,
He leadeth me beside the still waters.
He restoreth my soul; He leadeth me in the paths of righteousness
For His name's sake.
Yea, though I walk through the valley of the shadow of death,
I will fear no evil:
For Thou art with me.
Thy rod and Thy staff, they comfort me.
Thou preparest a table before me in the presence of mine enemies.
Thou anointest my head with oil, my cup runneth over.
Surely goodness and mercy shall follow me all the days of my life,
And I will dwell in the House of the Lord for ever.

23rd PSALM

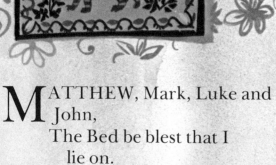

MATTHEW, Mark, Luke and
John,
    The Bed be blest that I
        lie on.
Four angels to my bed,
Four angels round my head,
One to watch, and one to pray,
And two to bear my soul away.

ALL good gifts around us
 Are sent from Heaven above,
So thank the Lord, O thank the Lord,
For all His love.

(J. Montgomery Campbell)

A Cowboy's Prayer

LORD, shield me from the blazing sun,
And let me find a water hole;
Protect me from the rustler's gun,
And dust storms in the desert bowl.
And when I reach the prairies' end,
Where dues are paid and comrades part,
Let me remember the Lord's my Friend
And thank Him with a grateful heart.

THANK you for the
world so sweet,
Thank you for the food
we eat,
Thank you for the birds
that sing,
Thank you, God, for
everything.

E. R. LEATHAM

BATS that flit,
Snakes that spit,
Rats and mice—
Not awfully nice;
Ugly toads, spotty frogs
Things that live in rotten logs.
In their cobwebs jewelled with dew,
Spiders, that seem ugly too.
Though for you they have no charm
Do not do them any harm.
Jesus loves them one and all,
He watches for them when they fall.
In spite of their unlovely features
Pity these who are God's creatures.

I SEE the moon, and the moon
sees me.
God bless the sailors on the sea.

DEAR God, be good to me;
The sea is so wide,
And my boat is so small.

(Breton fisherman's prayer)

THE SELKIRK GRACE

SOME hae meat, and canna eat,
  And some wad eat that want it;
But we hae meat and we can eat,
And sae the Lord be thankit.

ROBERT BURNS (1759-1796)

TEACH me, my God and King,
  In all things Thee to see,
And what I do in anything,
To do it as for Thee.

GEORGE HERBERT (1593 – 1633)

WHAT can I give Him,
   Poor as I am?
If I were a shepherd
I would bring a lamb;
If I were a wise man
I would do my part,
Yet what can I give Him?
Give my heart.
             CHRISTINA GEORGINA ROSSETTI
                       (1830—1894)

AWAY in a manger, no crib for a bed,
The little Lord Jesus laid down his sweet head.
The stars in the bright sky looked down where He lay,
The little Lord Jesus asleep in the hay.

The cattle are lowing, the Baby awakes,
But little Lord Jesus no crying He makes.
I love Thee, Lord Jesus! Look down from the sky,
And stay by my bedside till morning is nigh.

Be near me, Lord Jesus; I ask Thee to stay
Close by me for ever, and love me, I pray.
Bless all the dear children in Thy tender care,
And take us to Heaven to live with Thee there.

MARTIN LUTHER

O Jesus, I offer Thee this day
All my thoughts and work and play.
Let me be good as good can be,
Gentle, loving, kind like Thee.